Troubleshoot Smıu by
IT Troubleshoot:
Bart Tacken

Published by: Baɪ
Troubleshootsmarter.com
Copyright © 2021 Bart Tacken

All rights reserved. No portion of this book may be reproduced in any form without permission from the publisher, except as permitted by U.S. copyright law. For permissions contact: info@troubleshootsmarter.com

CONTENTS

Preface	2
Part 1 - Introduction to Troubleshooting	8
Attitude	10
The essential knowledge prerequisite	16
Analyze and diagnose	19
Recap	27
Part 2 – Troubleshooting Systems	28
Generic troubleshooting strategies	29
Mental Set	30
Trial and Error	32
Algorithmic	34
Heuristic	36
Solving problems with Basic Heuristics	38
Example #1: Users forget their passwords frequently.	39
Example #2: Slow Outlook client	41
Recap	42

Part 3 - IDEAL Problem Solving	44
1 – Identify the problem	46
Problem statement	47
Tool - 5W2H method	50
2 – Define the problem	56
Fishbone diagram	57
Five Times Why	61
3 – Explore Possible Solutions	63
What kind of solutions are out there?	64
Immediate solution	65
Permanent solution	66
Preventive solution	67
Brainstorm	68
Calculate risk	69
Compare solutions	71
4 – Anticipate and Act	73
SMART Goals	74
Risk mitigation	76
Planning	78
5 - Look and Learn	80
Look	81
Learn	82
Recap	83
Part 4 – In the Field	85

Common pitfalls	86
Signal vs. Noise	87
Assumptions vs. Conclusions	90
Troubleshooting wild cards	91
Binary Search	92
Google-Fu	96
Change Analysis	100
When you're stuck	102
Sending in the calvary	103
Rubber duck debugging	106
Occam's Razor	107
Aha! moment	109
Recap	110
Closing thoughts	111

PREFACE

Does your job require a lot of troubleshooting, but you've never had any training on the subject of solving problems?

Have you ever jumped into a problem, only to find out you've wasted a lot of time solving the wrong problem?

Maybe you have a lot of experience in troubleshooting but lack a straightforward method or strategy?

If you've answered "Yes" to any of these questions, this book is for you!

I'm sure most people reading this book will have a lot of field *experience* in troubleshooting. But how much do you really *know* about generic troubleshooting?

Wouldn't it be great if we could sharpen our troubleshooting saw for our day-to-day troubleshooting? Use some of the best tried and true information there is and start troubleshooting smarter, not harder?

Since I've started my IT career, I've always had a fascination for troubleshooting. Troubleshooting more intelligent was something I was thinking about for years.

I've got many years of training and other forms of education in IT, but there's very little attention given to troubleshooting.

Astonishingly, there's so little focus within the IT world on something we spent most of our time on; The process of troubleshooting and solving problems in any shape or form.

So, why haven't they taught us the nuts and bolts of troubleshooting?

For example, a lot of time during medical training is focused on medical diagnosing in the medical field. Trying to find out what disease or condition explains a persons' symptoms and medical signs.

But in IT, we tend to focus mainly on knowledge tied to specific products from vendors like Microsoft or Citrix.

Don't get me wrong, having the proper technical knowledge is very important and a prerequisite for effective troubleshooting, as we will learn. However, I think this has been driven too much by the IT certification industry, and we should be focusing more on acquiring *skills*.

An example of this would be the skill to search on the Internet versus memorizing (soon to be outdated) metrics.

Think about it. How much time of your day do you spend on solving problems in your job? I believe it's the elephant in the room; improving your troubleshooting skills will be a massive payoff for the rest of your entire IT career.

Furthermore, with rapid developments in Artificial Intelligence and automation, troubleshooting will become an increasingly critical future-proof skill!.

During my career, I've worked for different IT companies in various roles. And without exception, I noticed that most of the time, I was busy troubleshooting problems.

Generally, problems would eventually get solved. But at what expense?

- Troubleshooting sometimes took very, *very* long.
- After solving a problem, it would frequently return.
- Transferring an escalated problem was a disaster. I couldn't explain the problem or all the possible solutions I'd tried (even though I worked on it for hours).

It dawned on me that I didn't had a plan or strategy for troubleshooting. So, I just kept asking a bunch of questions on the fly and go from there.

Fortunately, I came across an article about solving generic problems. It opened a new perspective, and it made me realize that troubleshooting is a skill to *learn* and *improve*!

I ended up going down a rabbit hole in the process, going through books, blog posts, podcasts, and videos about getting better at troubleshooting.

However, I quickly realized there's an overwhelming amount of information available. It forced me to document the best stuff during this journey and, in the end, crammed all the essential stuff that works down in this book.

Some of the things you'll learn:

- Some Jedi mind tricks for troubleshooting
- What pieces of information are essential to solving every problem?
- A universal and easily accessible troubleshooting approach.
- Different cognitive strategies our mind uses for approaching problems.
- An evergreen problem-solving model for

solving complex issues.
- Various tools ranging from efficient brainstorming to calculating risk.
- Some proven troubleshooting wildcards.
- What a rubber duck has to do with troubleshooting?
- Different practical examples throughout the book.

Through this journey, I learned that troubleshooting is a *learnable* skill that you can develop. So, rather than covering each problem you might encounter in your IT role, this book will provide you with the knowledge and tools to get an edge in effectively troubleshooting any problem.

I hope you'll enjoy the book, forgive my bad jokes, and start kicking ass in troubleshooting!

PART 1 - INTRODUCTION TO TROUBLESHOOTING

One of the essential life skills is your ability to solve problems. Particularly in IT, the ability to effectively troubleshoot problems will come in handy each day for the rest of your career.

Most of us will encounter a wide range of different types of technical problems. How should we go about solving these kinds of issues? Is there a one size fits all approach?

Well, I discovered that there's a lot of overlap in the different types of troubleshooting strategies. But first, let's start with some of those troubleshooting basics that will help us understand each situation.

Many troubleshooting basics or strategies that seem obvious and trivial are often overlooked when implementing them. This is one reason there is value in endlessly returning to these fundamentals.

Some of the things we're going to learn in this part:
- Some Jedi mind tricks for troubleshooting.

- Why failing to plan is planning to fail.
- What pieces of information are essential to solving every problem?
- A universal and easily accessible troubleshooting approach

ATTITUDE

The result of your troubleshooting will depend significantly on your perception and attitude towards the problem at hand. Stress does not come from the situation on its own but primarily from the way you respond.

> *The problem is not the problem; The problem is your attitude about the problem.*

Realizing that the only part you can control is your attitude and actions towards the problem is *critical*. When you switch from a blaming mentality to a solution-oriented mentality, you're naturally starting to look for solutions.

A nice little Jedi mind trick for getting into a solution-oriented mindset is asking yourself, "How can I...?" This will let your brain naturally develop different ways to get to a solution. Your brain is the ultimate problem solver, and you just have to ask the right questions!

For example:

- How can I get more information about this error?
- How can I let the user print again?
- How can I get support?

Now try It yourself! How can I ...?

Focus on trying to spend your time and energy on the things you can control. In the best-selling book *"The seven habits of highly effective people,"* author Stephen Covey distinguishes the things we can control and the things we can't.

This distinction also relates to the problems we face each day. Stephen has a model that divides these into circles:

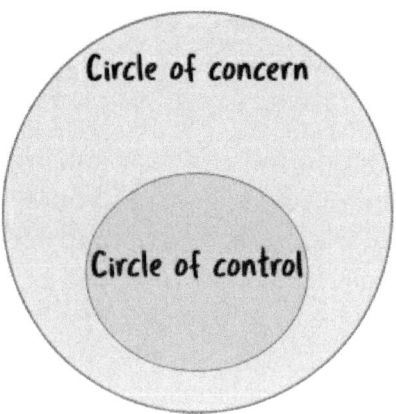

The *circle of concern* covers everything that affects

us. The *circle of control*, however, includes everything we have complete power over. For example:

- How we communicate (e.g., how to respond to an angry customer)
- How we follow up (e.g., level of detail, pace)
- Honoring agreements

Be aware to spent most of your time and energy on things within our circle of control.

Classic pitfalls to spend time on in the circle of concern:

- Playing the blame game
- Unable to accept a particular situation (e.g., argue about a piece of hardware a customer uses. Not just taking the case and start working toward a solution.)
- The behavior of an (angry) customer

Please don't fall into the trap of trying to change things we can't control. For example, finding a scapegoat won't change anything about the problem at hand.

Instead, use that creative energy and time for solving problems!

Having a plan

We all know that type of colleague that prepares a

configuration change down to the letter. Carefully written down each step, fallback plan, the whole nine yards.

Imagine you've been assigned the exact configuration change for a different device. Wouldn't it be great to get to work with that plan?

Having a plan will make you more confident and eager to get started with the actual configuration, and the same goes for troubleshooting complex problems.

This is one of the main reasons we will explore the IDEAL problem-solving model later in this book. This system can be used in particular when there are many moving parts or the huge impact of a problem.

But don't get me wrong, even handling day-to-day issues can benefit from a structured approach like starting with the same default steps or questions.

Still not convinced? Let's go through some benefits of having a prepared plan:

- Clarity

Some problems make you feel lost and overwhelmed, without knowing what to do to move forward. A plan will let you break down complex problems into smaller parts.

By breaking it down into smaller pieces, you'll get more overview and insight into prioritizing your time and energy.

- Save CPU power

Following a plan with specific steps will prevent us from reinventing the wheel each time. These steps will provide some structured guidance you can hold on to in the heat of the moment.

Also, following the direction of a plan will save some precious brain CPU power that we can use for creative problem-solving.

- Consistency

Following a well-thought-out plan prevents you from skipping essential troubleshooting steps. You'll appreciate this when you're under (time) pressure.

- Save time

A plan saves time by pointing out where to focus your energy and time. Furthermore, a thorough plan will focus on the permanent solution or even preventive solutions.

Thus, it's the ultimate time-saver, preventing

(the same kind of) problems.

THE ESSENTIAL KNOW-LEDGE PREREQUISITE

One of the most critical things with efficient troubleshooting is having enough knowledge about the system.

By that, I mean we must understand how to work with the system (inputs), what the system does (outputs), and how it does it (processes).

"Without knowledge, experience is blind."

I can't stress enough how important this is. Imagine you've got a problem with starting your car. The better you understand how the vehicle (system) works, the easier it will be to troubleshoot the problem.

Also, you can't troubleshoot if you don't know the inputs and outputs of a system. If you catch yourself asking, "Is it supposed to do that?". Chances are, you're not familiar enough with the system you're troubleshooting.

Take the example of a dishwasher that doesn't clean properly. You know how to operate it (inputs) and its purpose (outputs) but have no idea how it does it (processes).

In this example, I'm missing one out of three essential knowledge components necessary to troubleshoot the dishwasher problem; understanding the *processes*.

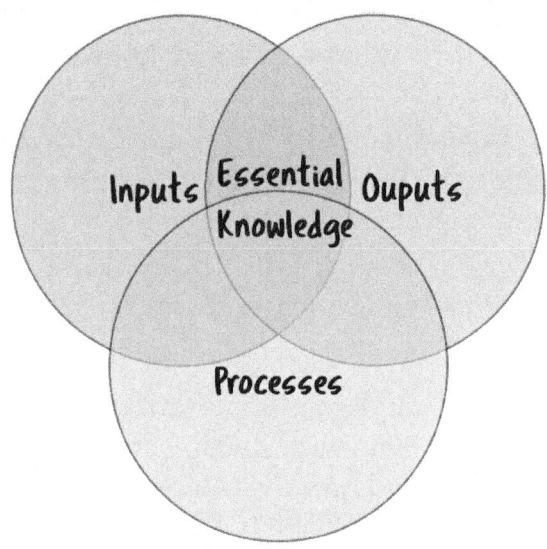

But would I've known how a dishwasher operates, I probably could tell what part should be cleaned or replaced first to solve the problem.

This is a common problem when troubleshooting. Most of us are jack-of-all-trades, knowledgeable in many technical areas but often lack the *depth* of knowledge.

Unfortunately, the troubleshooting methods we'll touch on won't replace the need for this knowledge. Remember to troubleshoot effectively; You must understand the inputs, outputs, and processes of the systems you manage.

ANALYZE AND DIAGNOSE

Now we know our requirements, let's discuss our troubleshooting approach. Let's take, for example, a printer problem.

As we discussed in the dishwasher example, inputs to the system generate specific outputs.

Any unexpected or undesirable behavior is a *symptom*. Frequently the symptom is a failure of the product or process to produce the expected result.

In our dishwasher example, dirty dishes after running the dishwasher are an obvious symptom of a faulty dishwasher.

To solve the problem, we will need to isolate the specific cause or causes of the symptom.

But how do we determine the cause? All the different troubleshooting methods and techniques out there have one thing in common, the process of *elimination*. I'm sure you're familiar with it. It's eliminating each possible cause until only one is left.

In this chapter, I'll lay down an easy-to-follow method that uses this process of elimination. This method consists of the following steps:

- Gather symptoms
- Ask questions
- Examining outputs
- Usual suspects
- Quick fixes
- Elimination

Gather symptoms

Regardless of the complexity of the problem, troubleshooting begins by gathering the problem's symptoms.

After gathering these, ask yourself what the output should be and where it differs from the current situation.

Ask questions

To gather more information about the problem, we need to ask questions.

Most of the time, we can pick the essential information with just a few basic questions that'll apply in about every situation:

- What happened? / What's wrong?
- What have you already tried?
- When did the problem first occur?
- What's the error message?
- Who is affected by this problem?

Examining outputs

After gathering all information, we need to figure out *which* outputs of the system are unusual.

For example, if a user tells you they cannot start application X. It's your job to figure out what part of the system has an unusual outcome and thus causes a problem.

We define the problem by investigating all aspects of the system and its outputs.

For example, can I still reach the server over the network? Is the application service still running?

Can I connect to the server that runs the database for this app?

Usual suspects

You've probably noticed that some components of a system are more likely to fail than others. Usually, these parts will have the most interactions, like moving parts in a physical device.

A printer, for example, will have a lot more issues with consumables like the ink toner cartridges and paper than with the power cable.

Another common cause of problems is user (or IT administrator!) interactions. If input data is not complete or accurate, the resulting output of the system will be unreliable.

When troubleshooting, being aware of these high probability causes will make you more effective and save you a lot of time!

Quick fixes

A fundamental principle in troubleshooting is starting to look for the simplest and most probable causes first.

Therefore, most helpdesk will tell you to reboot your system first before further looking into a problem because a lot of times, there are *quick fixes* available.

A quick fix sounds like a second-class solution. And it often is but can be very useful in restoring (partial) functionality, essentially buying you some time to investigate the problem further to get to the root cause.

Some examples of these quick fixes:

- Turn a device off and on again
- log out and in again
- Turn off the Anti-Virus software

Depending on the impact and how long it might take you to solve, you might want to put a *workaround* in place.

A workaround is a way to circumvent a problem. Like a quick fix, a workaround will minimize the impact of the problem, buy you some time, and reduce stress for you and the user.

Elimination

In our previous step, "Quick fixes," we've already started the process of elimination. Now, we want to start with an educated guess based on the answers to the questions we've asked.

Most of the time, there are more potential solutions. So how do we know which option to try first?

- **Use the fastest solutions first**

This way, you want to use the fastest solution first and testing those until you find the answer or isolate the (root) cause.

Imagine a weird software problem on a computer where a program won't start. In this case, you would restart your computer first before reinstalling the application because it's much faster to test if a restart will solve the problem.

- **Use the most straightforward explanations first**

Start with the most straightforward explanations first and testing those until you find the solution or isolate the root cause.

For example, take the weird software problem example. Ask yourself when the program performed well and what has changed since. Suppose it was the installation of a Windows update. The simplest explanation would be to deinstall this update and bring back the device in the same state before the problem.

In the end, we must compare the solutions against one another and select the one that will maximize the return on investment of our time/resources, and start eliminating possible causes until we've found our solution.

RECAP

We've learned that we should focus our efforts on the circle of control and thus the things we can control.

Using a method or system to work on a problem has many benefits. It will save us time and energy. Moreover, it gives a structured path toward a solution.

To solve a problem, we need to have the essential knowledge about an issue. This essential knowledge consists of understanding three necessary components of the system we're troubleshooting (inputs, outputs, and processes).

In a generic troubleshooting approach, finding a solution to a problem involves some elimination process. We've looked at an easy-to-follow method with the following steps:

- Gather symptoms
- Ask questions
- Examining outputs
- Usual suspects
- Quick fixes
- Elimination

In the next chapter, we will look at some generic troubleshooting strategies that our minds can use.

PART 2 – TROUBLE-SHOOTING SYSTEMS

There isn't a day that goes by where we don't have to solve some problem. But have you ever considered what approach you should take? Are there even different strategies out there? And, which questions should you ask?

This chapter will go through different problem-solving strategies our minds can use and find the pros and cons for each.

Some of the things we're going to learn in this part:

- Why we often don't have to think to solve a problem.
- Three basic troubleshooting approaches.
- A walkthrough on how to solve problems using a toolkit of heuristics.

GENERIC TROUBLESHOOTING STRATEGIES

When we're trying to solve a problem, we subconsciously implement some problem-solving strategy. Let's look at how our mind usually solves a problem and what troubleshooting strategies are out there.

MENTAL SET

Often, we don't actually have to solve a problem because we have a mental list of past solutions in our memory, and we simply have to bring the right one to mind.

For example, if someone asks you to add 5 + 5, you immediately know the answer. It takes no new thinking, and therefore you don't have to go through any problem-solving steps. But at some point, in the past, you did work to solve this problem.

This approach is called a *mental set*. It's a problem-solving approach that worked in the past but might not necessarily work for a new problem, but it's the first thing we try.

For example, imagine having fixed a computer problem in the past by restarting it. Your mental set now contains this proven solution, and therefore if you have a similar computer problem, you're likely first to restart the computer to solve this similar problem.

This is a very intuitive method for solving problems. Everyone will subconsciously go through a mental set when troubleshooting.

Keep in mind that this may not always work out

because your mind is trying to use old solutions for new problems. We often can't use our mental set and have to work through a problem with actual troubleshooting to get a solution.

Basically, all troubleshooting strategies make use of one of these approaches:

Strategy	Description	Examples
Trial and Error	Trying different solutions until a problem is solved	Restarting Windows computer, turning Bluetooth off and on again
Algorithmic	Step-by-step instructions to solve a problem	Instruction manual for installing software, cooking recipes
Heuristic	General problem-solving framework	Rule of thumb, Common sense, IDEAL method

TRIAL AND ERROR

Trial and error is a very basic approach to problem-solving and comes down to trying different solutions until the problem is solved. This strategy is usually done by people who have little knowledge about the issue at hand. A typical example of trial and error is a *brute force attack*.

During a brute force attack, a hacker tries to get access by trying many different combinations of usernames and passwords with the hope of eventually guessing correctly.

At first glance, this seems like an ineffective strategy, but it does help you explore what's called the *problem space*. The problem space are all parts that exist in the process of finding a solution to a problem.

Usually, most people will use a slight variation of the trial-and-error approach. Not just try any possible solution but only use the ones based on a *heuristic* like a *rule of thumb* or *common sense*.

This would turn a brute force attack into a *dictionary attack*, trying only variations of commonly used passwords.

Another example: imagine you're troubleshooting a broken printer. Using a refined trial and error approach, you would start with an educated guess and check if the printer isn't out of paper.

This is because there's more likely a problem with a highly consumable part rather than a more static part like a printer cable.

You'll learn more about heuristics later in this chapter.

ALGORITHMIC

Algorithmic strategies will provide you with step-by-step instructions to achieve a desired outcome.

"An algorithm guarantees that we'll get to a solution IF we follow all the steps."

The downside of algorithmic strategies is they tend to be slow because you must follow all the steps. Examples of algorithmic strategies are manuals or recipes. When you follow these closely, they will time and time again produce the same result.

For example, imagine you've lost your house keys. You could follow an algorithm like:

If my keys are somewhere in my house, the step-by-step procedure for finding them would be to start in one corner of the house and slowly look into every single location, expanding out from that corner until you've searched every inch of the house.

This approach will guarantee that you'll find the keys, but it's also very time-consuming and, therefore, won't be the way you're going to search for your keys. Because there are probably many places where it makes little sense to look for the keys, you're likely going to use a shortcut.

A heuristic approach would be to look in places where you remember having those keys the last time. This way, you can play the odds and save a lot of time.

However, if you don't find your keys, you might eventually resort to the algorithmic approach.

HEURISTIC

When confronted with a new problem, you're most likely not going to start with a rigidly structured problem-solving plan.

Instead, you probably use *heuristic techniques* to solve a problem quickly by finding an approximate solution and trading completeness or accuracy for speed.

You can think of heuristic techniques as mental shortcuts that help with the thinking processes in solving problems. These are usually hard-wired human behavior or learned informally, and we often use them unconsciously to solve a problem.

Heuristics apply known and generally applicable solutions. They don't *focus* on new solutions and limit creative thinking and innovation. Be aware of this when depending only on heuristics to solve a problem.

Some examples of commonly used heuristics:
- Educated guess
- Rule of thumb
- Profiling
- Common sense

- Stereotyping

For example, a problem where a user can't log in anymore and gets the error message "username or password is incorrect."

When using the *common sense* approach (a heuristic technique), our first question would be about the password. This is because common sense tells us passwords have to be changed periodically, and thus a forgotten password is much more likely to happen than a forgotten username.

Another everyday use for heuristics is in virus detection. You might not be sure a virus is there, but you can look for specific key attributes of a virus. Because the anti-virus software knows the characteristics of a typical virus, it will make an *educated guess* if we're dealing with a virus.

SOLVING PROBLEMS WITH BASIC HEURISTICS

Stanford University professor Jonathan Bendor has developed a basic toolkit for addressing issues using basic heuristics:

Decomposition	Starting small and divide the overarching problem into smaller pieces
Local search	Learn from prior experiences, look for known, similar solutions and adapt to them
Seriality	Going from point A to B. Make one small change first, then move on to the next
Multiple minds	Many hands make light work. Don't work on a problem alone. Find out what others think, and use them as resources.
Imitation	Don't try to reinvent the wheel. Find out what others are doing and copy them.
Recombination	Mix and match. Combine different ideas to come to a solution

This framework allows heuristics to be used in any order and repeatedly for different purposes as needed. This may sound impractical, but you'll find that they are really intuitive after using these several times. Let's look at some examples.

EXAMPLE #1: USERS FORGET THEIR PASSWORDS FREQUENTLY.

Problem: The service desk noticed that a lot of users keep forgetting their login passwords. This causes frustration for the users and adds additional load on the Servicedesk.

Problem-solving using basic heuristic toolkit:

Initially, the problem-solving group were Service desk employees. But later, the Servicedesk manager, some power users, and senior engineers got involved. (Multiple Minds)

This new problem-solving team asked users if there was a time the problem didn't occur and what has changed since. (Local Search). Also, the team started looking at other customers and how they've dealt with users that forgot their passwords frequently. (Imitation)

Alongside this, the problem-solving group will:

- Research the ticketing system when users tend to forget their passwords frequently.
- Look into ways a user can trigger a password reset.

(Decomposition)

The conducted research revealed that users are more prone to forget their passwords after a recent change in the password policy. The new password policy required the users to change their passwords more frequently and required longer and more complex passwords.

Other research showed that some customers use a password manager app that they access by fingerprint recognition on a mobile device. And other customers have Self Service password reset functionality implemented, so they don't have to contact Servicedesk for password-related problems.

After discussing the possible solutions with the customer, they decided to implement a password manager app. (Imitation)

EXAMPLE #2: SLOW OUTLOOK CLIENT

Problem: A customer is having a lot of issues with the performance of Outlook (An email client application).

Problem-solving using basic heuristic toolkit:

Ask the user when he experiences performance issues and if these problems also happen when working with the Outlook *web* client. It turns out the user only has a problem when starting the outlook client application. The performance of the Outlook web client works fine. (Decomposition)

You decide to compare the Outlook client configuration with the config of another user that doesn't experience problems. (imitation)

There are differences, but you're unsure which configuration setting decreases the performance, so you decide to start with the cache config setting. (seriality)

After changing this setting and starting outlook again, the user confirms that the startup speed is faster.

RECAP

So, we're aware now that solving *routine* problems is often just remembering a solution we've used in the past. We can use our mental set most of the time to use an old solution from the past that we can apply. This is the main reason why we often first try to power a device off and on again when there's a device-specific problem.

We've looked at using an algorithmic strategy for solutions. However, most of the time, we'll use a heuristic approach and attempt some sort of mental shortcut to solve the problem as fast as possible.

Reading about these core heuristics makes it look somewhat complex, but they're essentially the clichés of problem-solving. And with practice, you'll be able to recognize when to use which heuristic problem-solving strategy.

Nevertheless, they don't necessarily find a final solution, but they can quickly solve a problem by an immediate but temporary fix. If you're dealing with a more complex problem, you must rely on a more structured approach.

In the next chapter, I'll introduce the IDEAL (Identify, Define, Explore, Act, Look back) troubleshooting method. This method will allow for that structured approach.

PART 3 - IDEAL PROBLEM SOLVING

Have you ever noticed an increasing complexity in the problems you're facing during your career?

This complexity can express itself in many ways. Some examples of elements that make problems more complex are:

- Issues with intermittent symptoms
- Escalated problems where impact and stakes are high.
- Issues with apps or functionality that rely on different (third party) players.

As discussed, having a plan has many benefits. When dealing with complex issues, it helps to take a more structured approach. Of course, there are many frameworks for approaching problem solving out there. But most of them are by, and large the same and primarily differ on the level of detail.

As a busy IT professional, you want something practical and with as little overhead as possible. And that's where the IDEAL framework comes in. It's an evergreen problem-solving model, outlined by Bransford and Stein in their book, *The Ideal Problem Solver*, in 1984. The model consists of 5 steps that systematically work your way towards a solution.

The following graphic illustrates the steps we will cover:

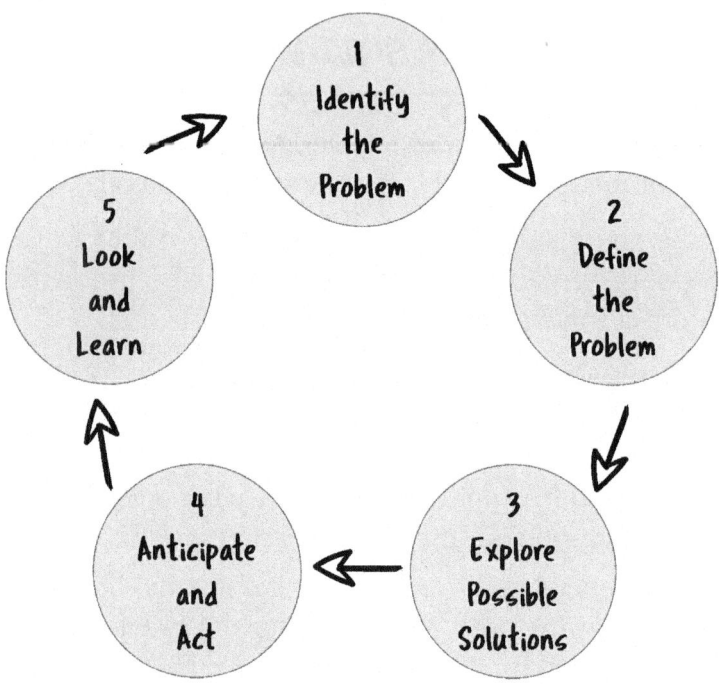

IDEAL is a flexible model that aids in generating creative solutions. Depending on the problem, with each step, you must assess how deep you want to dive in and spend time there. We'll also go through different tools and techniques available to zoom in and gather more insight and information for each stage.

1 – IDENTIFY THE PROBLEM

During my research, I've come across this quote. It's essential to solve a problem, so it should be this quote if you take anything away from this chapter.

> *"A problem well stated is half solved."*

We need to be able to identify and define the problem we're trying to solve. We can do this by creating a *problem statement.*

PROBLEM STATEMENT

Creating a problem statement will be one of the most critical steps in the process because if we're going after a symptom instead of the root cause, we'll waste a lot of time, and the problem will come back.

It's so tempting to jump right into a problem and neglect the definition of the actual problem to be solved. But I'm here to remind you this approach increases the risk of cracking the wrong problem. A (complex) problem cannot be decrypted if it's not entirely understood.

There's very much information on this topic alone, and constructing a problem statement quickly gets complex. But when you're in the field, you want to have a hands-on approach that's easy to understand. I'm a firm advocate of the *Keep It Stupid Simple* (KISS) principle and believe most systems work best if they are kept simple rather than complicated.

Problem statements can vary in length, depending on the complexity of the problem. But no matter what, it should be your goal to make it concise while clearly identifying the problem. The following is a simple hands-on template to use in everyday problem solving:

The issue	Describes the current state of the problem. It combines the answers we get from the questions we need to ask and contains the actions being done to attempt to solve the problem.
Objective	This describes the "to be" state of the problem and identifies the goals.
Consequences	This will describe the negative consequences resulting from the problem and will give us an idea about the priority of the problem. Negative consequences can be money, time, productivity, etc.

Following this format will result in a clear and easy-to-understand problem statement. An example of a well-written problem statement about a user login problem may look like this:

Issue: Starting today, a colleague cannot log in anymore. When she tries to log in, she gets the error message "unknown username or password."

She claims the password hasn't changed recently. And she is the only one in her department with this problem. She tried a few times to enter the password, but she keeps getting the same error message.

Objective: She needs to log in as soon as possible so she can start with her job.

Consequences: If she can't log in, she is not productive for the company.

You probably noticed that writing a problem statement for a common login problem would be overkill. Of course, that's perfectly fine when it's a routine problem that can be quickly solved.

But imagine having to hand over the problem because of an escalation. The problem statement would be of great help when briefing your colleague about the issue. Plus, a problem statement will also be handy in documenting the problem in a ticket registration system.

TOOL - 5W2H METHOD

Before we can write our problem statement, we must gather information and start asking questions. But where should we begin, and which questions should we ask to define the problem better?

> *"Having a good set of problem-solving questions prepared is a lot better than having none."*

The *5W2H method* is an efficient and easy-to-use tool that can help us get the correct information. At first glance, it may seem complicated, but it's really the exact opposite. The acronym represents the seven questions of the method.

Check out the simplified 5W2H table below with a brief explanation of all questions:

5W2H Question	Example	Description
What?	What's the problem? What's the input? What's the output?	Description of the issue
Why?	Why is it important to fix the problem?	Justification or reason for solving the problem
Where?	Where is the problem occurring?	Location of complaints (e.g. department, customers)
When?	When did the problem first occur? When does the issue occur?	The date and time problem was identified
Who?	Who is affected by the problem? Who is responsible for the hosting?	Individuals/customers associated with the problem
How?	How did the problem happen? How can the problem be reproduced?	Description of process
How Many?	How many times has this happened before?	Time and frequency of the problem

As you may have noticed, each step in the 5W2H method refers to a different question, and the answer to every question can trigger the next question.

Although I've presented these five questions in an order that seems logical, the approach will differ in practice.

Below are some general guidelines and ideas for using the 5WH2 method:

- Your first question should be an open-ended question that will let the user tell their story. For example, "What's the problem?" or "What happened?". Adding an additional question like "Can you explain it as clearly as possible?" will challenge the user to explain the problem best.

- By asking the question "Who is affected by the problem," we can better understand the type and urgency of the problem. For example, if multiple users are affected, odds are this isn't a user error and may be more urgent.
- You may need to revisit some questions. Answering one query will sometimes reveal essential aspects of other questions that you'd not yet considered.
- Don't force yourself to go through all the 5W2H questions if you feel it doesn't make any sense. For example, when you're dealing with routine problems.
- What have you already tried? The purpose of this question is to prevent duplicate work. But remember that the user could "forget" things. More savvy users/admins sometimes withhold information because they fear (or know) they just made the problem worse.
- Always ask for an error message. A clever shortcut in troubleshooting is searching for a particular error message.

Unfortunately, there isn't a top list of magical questions that will identify all problems. Just look at the ten most recent issues you've solved and determine the question relevant to the problem. I bet there's a wide variation.

Applying the 5W2H might not work for every situation, but it's a valuable tool to have at your disposal when you need some inspiration in gathering more information.

Ok, so now let's put this knowledge to work! We're going through a real-world example and walk through using the 5WH2 method to identify the problem:

Imagine performing an update for an application that's in use by the HR department. The update contains new templates for creating company policy guidelines.

However, during a functional test from an application administrator, he finds out all current templates are lost, and nobody can access documents based on these templates anymore.

First, we ask our questions:

- **What's the problem?**

An application update removed all document templates within the HR application. As a result, creating new policy documents is impossible. Furthermore, all documents based on these templates are inaccessible.

- **What's the error message?**

Both the update and the following test procedure did not reveal an error message.

- **What have you already tried?**

We've performed a restart of the application and

database server. However, the same problem persists.

- **Who is affected by the problem?**

All users from the HR department require this application for their day-to-day operations. All personnel within the company are also affected. They cannot consult various company policies anymore.

- **When did the problem first occur?**

Before the update, there were no problems in using the application. These problems started after the application update.

- **Where does the problem occur?**

The problem occurs within the HR department application.

- **Why is this a problem? (impact)**

Our 5 HR employees can't do their job anymore, and all employees can't look into company policies anymore.

- **How? How did the problem happen? (Root cause)**

The problem happened when updating the HR application.

- **How many times has this problem already occurred?**

Previous updates never caused any problems.

After asking these questions, we can formulate a problem statement:

Issue: An update of the HR application removed all the document templates.

Objective: We want to restore the missing templates so our HR department can perform their daily tasks again and all employees can look into the company policies again.

Consequences: HR users cannot perform their daily tasks anymore. Employees of the company cannot access the various company policies anymore.

As you can tell from the example, we can get a good overview of the problem by asking the 5WH2 questions!

But remember, the 5W2H tool isn't a one-size-fits-all question generator but a systematic approach for basic troubleshooting questions to help you get started. Extend the list of questions with other ones based on the unique needs of your problem.

2 – DEFINE THE PROBLEM

In this step, we're going to start diagnosing the problem. We'll be going to use two time tested tools for digging deeper into issues:

- Fishbone diagram
- Five Times Why

Complex problems are like puzzles with pieces that interconnect and overlap. This can make it difficult to separate symptoms from the underlying root cause(s).

> *"Finding the root cause is critical because it means that you're able to prevent an issue from happening again."*

These tools will help us in finding the underlying cause, also known as the *root cause*. To find these root cause(s), we need to put our thinking caps on. The *Fishbone diagram* can help us brainstorming for possible reasons.

FISHBONE DIAGRAM

Often a picture or graph can convey an idea more quickly and effectively than the written word. In particular, complex information can be easier to understand when presented in a visual form.

"A picture is worth a thousand words."

Mind mapping is an excellent example of this. A visual representation will generate more ideas and identify relationships between different information.

Another example is a *fishbone diagram*. A fishbone diagram is a visual tool for effective *brainstorming* and can help us think about and categorize the different factors that may have led to the problem. This results in a more thorough *exploration* of the issues behind the problem.

Essentially, it's a variation on a mind map where the head of the fishbone diagram represents the problem, and the skeleton's backbone connects the spines representing different categories. These categories can have different sub-categories with likely causes.

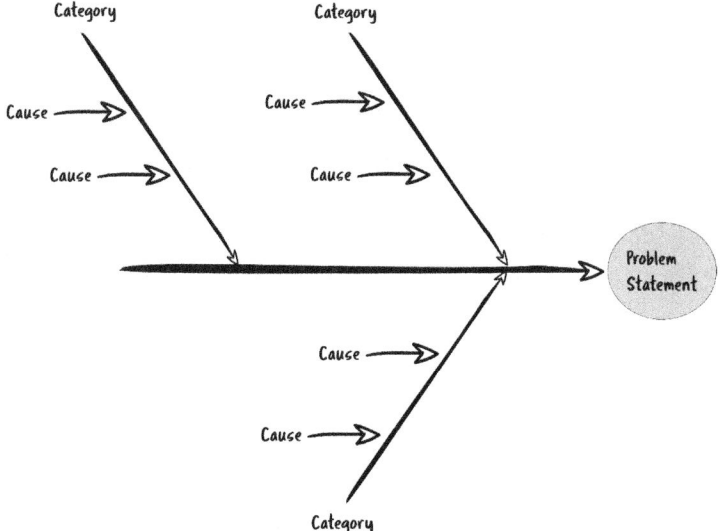

Let's make this more tangible with an example. Suppose you're having a problem with a company website that regularly crashes.

First, we're going to create our problem statement:

The issue: Since the weekend, our company site intermittently crashes. There hasn't been a change with this website or any underlying soft- or hardware in weeks. To solve the problem, we've already tried to reboot the server.

Objective: Have the website running reliably again.

Consequences: When the website is down, customers won't be able to find us online. This will lead to missed opportunities and bad publicity.

Next, we're starting to brainstorm for possible causes by going through 4 steps:

1. State the problem.
2. Define the categories to brainstorm on.
3. Brainstorm each category.
4. Analyze the results.

Let's go through these steps:

1. First, state the problem.

In this example, we like to know why the company website crashed.

2. Define the categories to brainstorm.

Just start with some categories that will come to mind and add or change along the way. So, in this example, we could come up with three types:

- Hardware: To catch causes related to the (underlying) hardware
- Software: To obtain reasons related to (underlying) software.
- Human: To obtain human faults related to the unreliability of the website.

3. Brainstorm each category and develop a list of best ideas about what may have caused the website to crash.

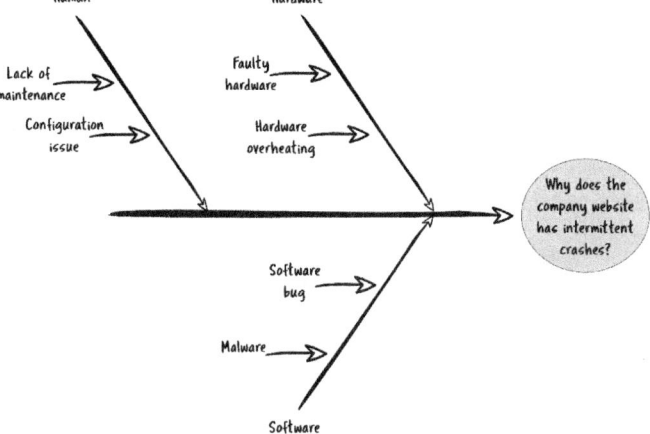

4. Analyze the results.

As you brainstorm all causes category by category, you could update the fishbone diagram.

To validate possible causes, you can ask whether removing that cause would prevent the problem. If the answer is yes, you may have found the (superficial) problem.

However, to get to the root of the problem, we have to use another great tool; the *Five Times Why* technique.

FIVE TIMES WHY

At this point, we should have an overview of the possible causes why the website crashed. Then, for each potential reason, we could start an investigation.

Start with investigating the most likely causes until you've found the right one. For example, suppose the reason the website crashed was an unpatched software bug. Was the root issue the missing patch, or is there some more structural issue at the root? After all, we want to deal with this problem once and for all!

Most of the time, problems are symptoms of deeper issues. To get to these deeper issues, we must take an extra step to find the root cause. The *Five times why* technique is one of the most effective tools for root cause analysis and will help us find the root cause of any problem.

Basically, this works by keep asking *why* until you get to the root of the problem. You'll be surprised to find out how powerful this tool can be!

We've found out a specific error message pointing to a bug in the webserver software. So, let's take the five times why approach to get to the root cause:

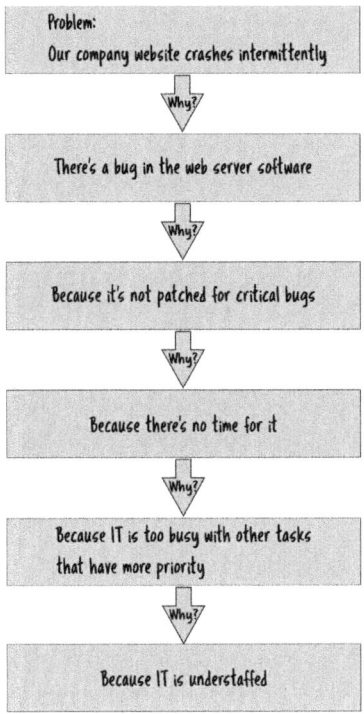

We used "why" five times to find our root cause; IT is understaffed. Notice how the five whys shifted our thinking and forced us to look deeper into the issue.

When applying the five whys, you'll often not like the answer, and that's fine. This is because the root cause in many cases is not technical but instead related to a budget, business process, or communication error.

3 – EXPLORE POSSIBLE SOLUTIONS

After we've identified the root cause, it's time to brainstorm and develop potential solutions. Often, there are a variety of possible solutions in which we can address the problem. We'll look at how we can efficiently brainstorm for these solutions, what different kinds of solutions are out there, and when to use them.

Of course, we want to consider the most straightforward solutions first and avoid jumping into complex or time-consuming solutions unless we must. However, this will require us to compare the different solutions against each other. But first, we look at the different kinds of solutions we can apply.

WHAT KIND OF SOLUTIONS ARE OUT THERE?

We all know not all solutions have the same quality and durability. Imagine a slow computer. Obviously, there's a difference between restarting the computer to alleviate the slowness versus upgrading the computer with better hardware.

So, let's look at the different kinds of solutions out there and where they differ.

IMMEDIATE SOLUTION

An immediate solution is where we quickly reduce the impact of the problem for the customer/user. In many cases, this immediate solution will buy us more time to investigate the root problem.

We can split immediate solutions into either a *workaround* or a *temporary fix.*

A workaround is a quick way to restore functionality to a usable level. For example, if an app is down, that's used for reporting a crime. The workaround could be for citizens to send an email to the police with details of the incident.

A temporary fix, in this case, would be to restart the back-end systems of the app to bring it up again. We don't know why the app crashed, but this immediate rebooting action will cause the app to be available again until the next outage.

The immediate action should only be temporary and not stay in place after the root cause is corrected. Quick fixes may seem convenient, but they often solve only the surface issues and waste resources that could otherwise be used to tackle the actual cause.

PERMANENT SOLUTION

The permanent solution will be the actions taken to eliminate the problem. It's a corrective action that will prevent the root cause from recurring. But unfortunately, this is where most people stop.

A permanent solution prevents the *same problem* from recurring but won't stop us from the same *kind* of problem happening again.

Let's retake our example of the app. It turns out the problem is related to the absence of critical operating system patches that came out last month.

The permanent solution would be to install those patches to prevent this problem from happening again. The permanent solution will resolve the *same* issue for that specific bug but won't prevent outages due to other software bugs requiring other patches installed.

PREVENTIVE SOLUTION

A Preventive solution is proactive and often changes *the process* to prevent the same kind of problem from recurring. This will prevent us from having the same *sort* of problem happening again.

In our example, a preventive solution could be to add a periodic patching process to ensure all critical patches are reviewed monthly and installed.

This would prevent the same kind of problem (bugs due to lack of critical patches) from happening again.

Another example showing the difference between permanent versus preventive solutions:

- Permanent solution: Train Servicedesk employees to deal with customer complaints.
- Preventive solution: Make incident intake training required for new employees working on the Servicedesk.

BRAINSTORM

To develop different solutions, we must get creative again. Typically, you would generate several viable solutions and screen them for feasibility. The more possible solutions you can come up with, the more likely it is to develop the ideal solution.

To help us generate ideas, we can use the following techniques:

- Brainstorming

This technique encourages everyone involved to spontaneously come up with solutions without overthinking them and fear of criticism. Brainstorming allows for *out-of-the-box* (farfetched) answers to surface.

- Visualization

As discussed earlier, a fishbone diagram is a tool for effective brainstorming. It can help us think about and categorize different things. In addition, the visual representation will generate more potential solutions and identifies the relationships between them more easily.

CALCULATE RISK

With every action we take in life, there's risk involved.

Change = Risk

Risk is not necessarily a bad thing. For example, we can analyze and accept certain risks. Just be aware of the amount of risk you're exposed to when performing corrective action. But how can we define the amount of risk?

In straightforward terms;
Risk = likelihood x consequence

Suppose we want to apply software patches to an application, and you want to get a better sense of the associated risk.

In the first scenario, let's assume we're patching a *redundant* server with *one-year-old* patches.

The likelihood of these patches still having problems after they were already released a year ago is low. A consequence of a faulty patch could be losing the functionality of the redundant server. However, this wouldn't impact the functionality of the app that's running on top of it. At worst, the performance would take a hit.

Likelihood = low
Consequence = low

Compare this example with installing patches on a *single* server with *new* patches.

In this case, the likelihood of these patches having teething problems is high. And because the server isn't redundant, the consequence would also be increased. Because when this server stops working after installing the patches, the app will stop running.

Likelihood = medium
Consequence = high

These examples show a straightforward way to determine the risk involved in a corrective action. We use this easy formula to determine the risk for each potential solution and consider it when comparing solutions to decide which one's best.

COMPARE SOLUTIONS

Once we've got all possible solutions, we need to compare solutions against each other and select the best one. To compare these solutions, I prefer to make use of a pros and cons list. Then, just list out the advantages and disadvantages so you can make an informed decision.

Below is an example of a basic pros and cons list:

Problem: Company website crashes

Immediate Solution: Restart Server

Pros	Cons
Doesn't require a lot of time and effort	Doesn't prevent the problem from coming back
Quickly restores functionality	When problem comes back, could be more often and/or severe

Permanent Solution: Apply patches

Pros	Cons
Will solve this problem once and for all	Installing software patch requires time and work
	Increased risk of downtime during patching

Permanent Solution: Periodic patching process

Pros	Cons
Will prevent the same kind of problems	Requires a patch process being put in place

You could also use a SWOT analysis, but I don't think the added complexity outweighs the added value.

When we compare these potential solutions, we need to consider the return on investment of time and resources. Often a solution for a problem is a sum of these different tradeoffs.

For example, cost vs. quality is a typical tradeoff. Consider restarting a system occasionally vs. reinstalling the operating system software on that system.

We should try to play the long game here and sacrifice some more time and effort in the short term by sticking to a permanent solution. Ideally, you want to have a preventive solution also in place.

Time passes quickly, and chances are few. After solving a problem with (huge) impact, you may find yourself having some more leverage, more than usual, to push our preferred solution through.

Seize these moments to make hay when the sun's out.

4 – ANTICIPATE AND ACT

Once we have our solution, we need to set a SMART goal and make a solid game plan. We've discussed risk in step three. Now it's time to think about risk mitigation and the specific measures we'll need to prepare.

Never a dull moment in IT. A Lot of times, we have a million things on our minds. This makes it easy to forget what we need to do to finish our work. Instead of using a full-blown project management tool, I'll lay out the case for using a basic checklist that we can use to monitor progress and provide an overview of our tasks.

I'm a firm believer of the KISS (Keep It Stupid Simple) principle. Therefore, I'll lay out the case for using a basic checklist.

SMART GOALS

How do we know if we achieved our goal? Well, we can make use of *SMART* goals. SMART is an acronym for the following characteristics:

- **S**pecific
- **M**easurable
- **A**chievable
- **R**elevant
- **Ti**me-Bound

There's very much information about SMART goals out there. Therefore, I don't want to bore you with all the details. The gist of SMART goal setting is these characteristics are excellent criteria for setting verifiable goals and bring structure into objectives.

Let's talk about our example of patching an app and turn it into a SMART goal:

Goal: Within this week I will patch servers APP01 and APP02 with critical patch XYZ	
Specific	The goal of patching the server with patch XYZ is well defined
Measurable	Success can be measured by looking up the installed patches on the servers
Achievable	Patch XYZ is compatible with the version of the application and they're available for download
Relevant	Applying this patch would solve the problem at hand
Time-bound	There is a deadline set when these patches will be installed

RISK MITIGATION

When we were exploring different solutions, we'd also perform a quick risk analysis. In this step, we're going to deal with the risks involved. Dealing with these risks is also called *Risk mitigation*.

Risk mitigation is a strategy to prepare for and lessen the effects of threats. In our case, these threats are negative implications of our problem-solving actions.

Let's go back to our example of patching the app. When applying new patches, there's always a risk that changing application code can introduce other problems like preventing the application from starting up again.

For each corrective action, we need to create a risk mitigation plan. Don't be scared by the fancy name. Just make a list of all the possible risks you can come up with and what you can do about it.

Some examples of typical risk mitigation steps are:

- Check if there is a valid backup in place and prepare what it takes to restore it in advance.
- Prepare configuration steps for a rollback if needed.
- Check the possibility to contact a (software)

vendor after business hours during the corrective action.

Of course, you won't forget these risk mitigation measures before performing corrective actions. But just to make sure, make it a part of your IDEAL checklist.

PLANNING

It's easy to forget all the things we need to do to complete a set of tasks. We need some way to track our progress and provide an overview of our tasks.

How you choose to monitor progress will depend on the nature and complexity of the goal. When working in a team and dealing with a complex interdisciplinary problem, you'll probably need some project management tool.

Such a tool will let us monitor our execution towards the main goals through sub-goals or milestones. We can use these to convert a complex goal into a full-blown project.

> *"Failing to plan is planning to fail."*

Great, but they're generally also very complex to set up and maintain. Trying to minimize overhead as much as possible, I'm a huge proponent of using checklists. Checklists are a simple tool that can help improve the effectiveness of individuals or groups.

Example of a checklist for patching the application:

Example of a checklist for patching an application	

Preparation	+ Read release notes
	  - Check software and system requirements
	  - Check supported upgrade path
	  - Check fixed and known issues
	  - Check new features
	  - Check installation steps (if any)
	+ Test Patches on a test server
	+ Take appropriate action to prevent false positives from a monitoring solution
	+ Check if the server backup is working

Execution	+ Reboot the server once before installing patches + Create a snapshot + Install patches + Reboot server
Test & Validate	+ Login on server and check (event) log + Test functionality by logging in with a test account and making use of the app. + Let customer (contact) know that patch installation was successful + Update ticket/call within the ticket registration system. + Remove snapshot next business day when the app keeps working fine.

Looking at this action list, it's becoming evident that we need to do the most work upfront. Inevitably, preparation is by far the essential part in this case. It may seem cumbersome at first, but some of us seasoned IT pros know good preparation will be invaluable more often than not.

5 - LOOK AND LEARN

In this last step, we'll evaluate the effects of the solution(s) applied. First, we must verify if the problem has been fixed AND hasn't broken something else. After solving the problem successfully, we must look back and review the analysis and look at the lessons learned.

As a final step, we need to document our solution to share this knowledge and prevent our colleagues from reinventing the wheel.

LOOK

We're going to evaluate and determine the extent to which the problem is solved.

First, we must return to the beginning and look at the initial symptoms or effects that started our troubleshooting journey to begin with.

If these symptoms aren't alleviated, and the effects are still present, our solution is ineffective, and we must revisit our problem-solving process.

Again, let us return to our app that needs patching:

Problem Solved!?	
Are the symptoms still present after we applied our solution?	No, the symptoms (unexpected crashes) did not arise anymore after appying our solution (installing the critical patches)

LEARN

If the problem is solved and the dust is settled, we need to review the analysis. What could we do better next time? And how can I make sure we don't make the same mistakes again?

A best practice is to set up a dedicated document about the troubleshooting journey and divide it into the IDEAL troubleshooting steps. Then, for each problem you've solved through the IDEAL method, write down an important thing you've learned solving this problem.

For example, maybe you've discovered a new tool that we can use during future problem analysis.

Also, don't forget to document the steps that lead to the solution in your ticket registration system. Would the problem arise again, we now don't have to rely on our memory solely, but we can look up what actions were taken last time to solve the problem.

It's a good idea to also document this in a manual so that others can apply it. This way, we share knowledge and transform the issue into an algorithmic problem that we can solve by following the manual.

RECAP

To guard against increasingly complex problems, we can make use of the IDEAL model. The model consists of five steps that systematically work your way towards a solution.

The first step in this model is to identify the problem. We can do this by creating a problem statement. For this problem statement, we first need to gather the correct information. The 5W2H tool is a tool that can help us get this information.

The next step is defining the problem. In this step, we're going to start looking for the root cause. The fishbone diagram can help us brainstorming for possible reasons. We need to investigate the most likely causes until we find the right one and dig deeper with the Five times why tool to get to the root cause.

After identifying the root cause in the second step, it's time to brainstorm and develop potential solutions. We explore the different types of solutions and try to assess the risk for each one. Finally, compare the possible solutions against each other by using a pros and cons list.

Step four requires us to set out SMART goals and make a solid game plan. This requires some risk mitigation. Risk mitigation measures will lessen the effects of threats. Now it's time to put everything together and start planning. To minimize overhead, we'll just use a good old checklist.

In our last step, we'll evaluate and determine the extent to which the problem is solved. Finally, we look back to evaluate the analysis.

PART 4 – IN THE FIELD

This chapter is about getting our hands dirty with practical stuff that can help us in the field. We'll be going through some of the best tips and tricks I've picked up over the years.

We'll first go over some common pitfalls to look out for regarding all the information we need to manage. Then we'll look at some troubleshooting wildcards and share some of the best tools to fight problems.

Finally, we're going over some things you can do when there seems no way out and you're stuck.

COMMON PITFALLS

SIGNAL VS. NOISE

Can you imagine troubleshooting IT problems without the Internet? Neither can I!

There's a wealth of information about virtually any topic you can find. Suppose you have a problem that generates some error message, or you're good at describing the problem with a few words into a search engine. There's a good chance someone else already solved this exact problem and documented a solution in a blog or something similar online.

Since the advent of the Internet, information is abundant and easy to access. Anyone who's ever searched on the Internet knows this. It's a blessing and a curse at the same time.

Information sometimes feels like a drug. It's very tempting to fall into a *rabbit hole* and mindlessly scroll different feeds. From a historical perspective, this makes sense.

The more information our ancestors had, the more likely they were to survive. But in the world of the Internet, we're exposed to an abundance of information. In this information overload, we must retake control and make the distinction between *signal* and *noise*.

In simple terms, signal is good, and noise is bad. Signal is the meaningful and relevant information you're trying to detect. Noise is random information that has no use and makes it harder to focus on the signal.

In *Fooled by Randomness*, Nassim Taleb argues that the noise-to-signal ratio increases as you consume more data. Humans tend to think more information leads to better decision-making. However, this usually leads to a high noise-to-signal ratio and more confusion.

Let's look at some examples:

Other people's opinions are usually a source of noise, I've found. This is particularly the case when there's a problem being escalated and handed over to you. There's a tendency for people to blow issues out of proportion and suddenly question all kinds of systems or processes that have been operating fine for years.

In this case, the noise would be a (one-off) incident and the signal how often this has happened in the last months.

Another example would be a problem that affects the internal mail flow of all users.

The signal, in this case, would be to look at recent changes for systems that are part of this internal mail flow. The noise would be to start questioning the whole IT environment instead and look for ways to update it.

To achieve a high signal-to-noise ratio, focus on the problem at hand and try to be selective about the information you're going to work with.

ASSUMPTIONS VS. CONCLUSIONS

An important distinction that any effective troubleshooter must make is about a*ssumptions* vs. *conclusions*.

As discussed earlier in this book, it's a default human strategy to use your *mental set* and make an assumption about a particular possible cause. This is a very intuitive method for solving problems. Everyone tends to distort facts to suit a specific narrative. This is a common pitfall, don't make up your mind before looking at the facts.

Imagine a problem with a server from a vendor with a bad reputation due to hardware problems.

Although a faulty memory module could certainly cause a Blue Screen of Death (BSOD), we generally need to have proof first before we're going to order a new module. Because in reality, all kinds of things like a software bug or a configuration issue can trigger a BSOD.

You can certainly have a theory, but it can't be baseless. Not based on preexisting prejudice, anecdotal evidence, or emotion but *actual facts*.

TROUBLESHOOTING WILD CARDS

BINARY SEARCH

You can think of any IT system or process in general as a whole made of different components. If one of these components doesn't work correctly, this often causes a problem for the entire system.

In troubleshooting, we must find out what component broke and what causes the problem. A very effective strategy for finding out is using a *process of elimination*. An intuitive method that works by eliminating one possible cause at a time until only one is left.

An excellent technique for speeding up this elimination quest is called *Binary Search*. It's a basic algorithm used to find an item in an array. This technique will systematically isolate the source of an issue. You may be familiar with its use in programming.

The basic idea is to narrow down the cause by splitting up the problem. Then, repeatedly asking if the issue occurs before this point until eventually, you find the spot where the issue occurs after but not before.

Let's take an example where a user is reporting that a specific website has a bad performance.

After checking the high probability causes (like restarting the Internet browser or laptop), we can start with writing down what infrastructure components are needed to browse on the website like below:

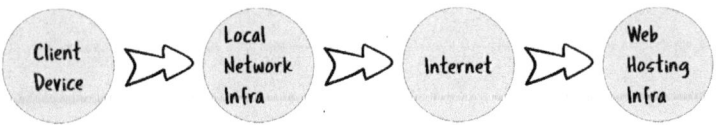

All these components are necessary, and each component's output relies on each other to let a user browse a particular website. When one of these components fails or suffers from performance issues, this could be a bottleneck and degrade the browsing experience.

Because we're going to repeatedly half the list of possible faulty components until we find the one that causes the issue, we start somewhere in the middle. Usually, there's some apparent logical divide you can make.

An obvious start would be to test between the Internet and the website hosting Infrastructure component in this example. Notice that this isn't in the middle but still is a fast way of eliminating components. We can test by browsing on other websites and determine if they have the same performance issues.

Suppose other websites don't have performance issues. In that case, you'll immediately know that every component up to the website hosting infrastructure part works well, and therefore the problem should be in the *website hosting* infrastructure component.

In case other websites also have performance issues, you would end up with the following components:

A quick test is to ask if more users experience the same problem. If other users share the same problem, we can remove the client device from the list.

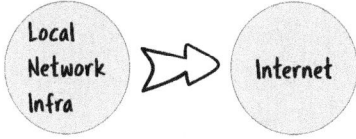

Now we're just left with two possible causes. We could attach a laptop to the Internet router to split this list and determine if this solves the performance problem. If this is the case, then the issue should be somewhere within the local network infrastructure.

Now we can start the same binary search for all the local network infrastructure components to find the problem component.

Should we be left with the client device, then this

search is probably not over yet. Within the client device is another layer with components that are necessary for browsing a website and could be causing a problem:

Now we have to start our binary search again until we find the problem.

Using this technique will speed up your troubleshooting tremendously instead of just eliminating one single component each time.

While it may not seem like much of a time saver for this example, imagine troubleshooting a system with 20 or 50 different components and how much time you could save!

GOOGLE-FU

Couldn't find it on the web? Son...
Your Google-Fu is weak.

Let's face it, in IT are your Google (Internet search) skills of crucial importance. Moreover, searching the Internet is one of the essential skills in troubleshooting. Who hasn't been sick of plowing through a stack of irrelevant information?

Stop wasting hours searching for answers, and let's explore some tips and tricks to improve your search game in the field.

Quotation marks

Use this when you're searching for a specific phrase. Using quotation marks is very useful when searching for that exact sentence, like a particular error message. Ensure to remove detailed information like user account names, IP addresses, or any data related to your specific environment.

Error messages with specific information tied to the customer environment will prevent you from just about all search results when using quotation marks.

Example: "An error occurred when attaching

the database. Event 1743"

Exclusion operator

This will exclude a term from your search and can help you filter your search results upfront. For example, when you want to exclude a specific software version.

The search term below will give you results on how to remove duplicates for Excel, excluding the Office Excel 365:

Example: Excel how to remove duplicates -365

Command Site:

This limits the search to within a specific website. Sometimes you want to search some trusted sites first before diving into the more obscure parts of the Internet.

This command can be handy if you wish to search within a specific forum or vendor support website.

Example: site:support.hp.com HP Elitebook 850 BSOD Driver_IRQL_Not_less_or_Equal

Command Cache:

Have you ever found a promising search result but couldn't browse the website due to a website not existing anymore or other access errors? If you're lucky, the website was indexed before the site became inaccessible.

You can find the cached version of the site by using the cache command combined with the site URL that's not accessible anymore.

Example: cache:linuxatemyram.com

Only use important words

A search engine takes your search phrase and matches it with keywords on websites. At the risk of sounding obvious, limit your search to include only essential words.

Using too many words generates irrelevant results. Take, for example, a problem with users logging in:

Don't use: Our users cannot log in due to an error in the log with error 43234.

Use: user cannot log in event log error 43234

Search the right source

When you're searching online, be aware of your sources. For example, when I have many search results to go through, I'm first looking for hits on blog posts. This is because blog posts are generally thoughtfully written with a clear layout of all steps to take.

Another reason I prefer these above official sources like a vendor's website is that they are primarily concise.

Vendors will tend to bombard you with information

making these articles very tough to follow through. Always keep an eye out for accuracy, though.

For instance, you can verify the gist of a particular blog post by skimming the vendor's official site on that exact topic.

CHANGE ANALYSIS

Generally, problems or failures are a result of a change that somehow touches the problem. Therefore, a valuable method to find a cause is to analyze the changes leading up to the problem.

This can be done by going through the following steps:

> 1. List out every change in chronological order that could be a potential cause.

Depending on the type of problem, you must decide how long you want to go back to analyze these changes.

Let's say the problem we're going to analyze is the outage of the crime reporting app. We want to view changes regarding the app and dependencies two weeks before the first time we had the problem.

> 2. Then we would have to categorize each change with a date. If you have many changes to go through, you could add a number representing the likelihood the problem is related to the root cause.

Date	Change	Related to root cause
01-01-2021	Updated the Operating System	1
14-01-2021	Expanded the virtual harddrive of the virtual server	3

WHEN YOU'RE STUCK

SENDING IN THE CALVARY

Sometimes problems are too complex or urgent to fix on our own. So, yes, you need help!

These kinds of problems will require us to send in the cavalry by escalating the problem. From experience, I can tell this can be a very tricky part of troubleshooting.

Usually, it requires clear communication, precision, and understanding of politics.

If you're anything like me, you'll want to solve all problems by yourself and think twice before asking for help from others. This is the first tricky part of the escalation process.

You must be honest and assess if you can deliver a solution on time or escalate a problem so other colleagues can get involved.

It depends on the problem, of course, but the two leading escalation indicators for me are:

- **Progress**

    Is there still progress being made?
- **Impact**

How significant is the impact if this doesn't get fixed fast?

A proper escalation is more than just calling your manager and telling him you need some help as soon as possible. I had my fair share of escalations. Below I've described the most important tips and tricks I've learned over the years.

Understanding

Especially in situations where a user is agitated, find an appreciation for their perspective. It's important to acknowledge the importance of the problem and show understanding. This way, you can diffuse the situation, and the user doesn't need to go against you and get more emotional.

Vigilant

You'll encounter some problems that have a higher likelihood of escalating. For example, the issues where *Very Important Persons* (VIPs) are involved. Think of executives, (senior) secretaries, or expensive external agents.

The same goes for the *type* of problem, like problems with impact on production. Ranging from a stagnant assembly line to users that cannot log in and conduct their work.

Communicate

Ensure all stakeholders (the affected users, for example) are aware the problem is escalated, to whom, and within which time frame you'll expect to contact the user about the status.

I've experienced several times the importance of this. It's critical to be upfront and transparent about status updates. Especially in those tricky escalations when there's a significant (production/financial) loss at stake.

Try to put yourself in their shoes. I know I would like to have someone be ruthlessly honest and transparent about the current status and game plan to solve the problem.

Log

Keeping a log and writing key actions down that you took during troubleshooting will help you prove you did the right thing at the right time and, for example, haven't waited too long before escalating.

Also, when things escalate, you want to have your facts straight! Know what part of the system works and doesn't, an overview of all steps taken to solve the problem, results, etc. These will give the new team a good head start.

RUBBER DUCK DEBUGGING

Rubber duck debugging? Are you kidding me?

No

Ok, you don't need a rubber duck, to be honest. I'm sure we all had the experience where you're explaining to a colleague the problem you're trying to solve and suddenly having an *Aha! moment*.

This moment doesn't have to be the final breakthrough but often will take you a step further in the problem you're dealing with. Think of a basic test you haven't done yet or some brilliant question you forgot to ask a user.

This is also known as *rubber duck debugging*: Explaining a problem to a rubber duck or someone or something else who doesn't have a clue about the problem.

It helps because you have to think about the problem differently to explain it to the rubber duck. And that's often when the issue reveals itself.

OCCAM'S RAZOR

Ever heard of *Occam's Razor*?

With increasing complexity in IT systems, the simplicity of Occam's Razor can be invaluable. Occam's Razor is a classic problem-solving principle.

The "razor" refers to "shaving away" of irrelevant stuff and assumptions. Occam's Razor states that the one with the fewest necessary assumptions should be right when you're weighing alternative theories. In plain English, the simplest solution is often the right one.

Ok, hold your horses here! This doesn't mean the most straightforward answer is *always correct*. It only suggests that, among all possible answers to a question, one's best pick would generally be the one that requires the least assumptions.

Still not sure what I mean? Let's take at some examples of Occam's Razor at work:

A server unexpectedly went down
   Likely – Someone accidentally chooses to shut down the server instead of logging out.
   Unlikely - The server was hacked.

A user cannot log in
   Likely – User forgot username or password.

Unlikely – The account was deleted.

Treat it like a rule of thumb that can guide you when choosing between different theories like the causes of a problem.

AHA! MOMENT

Often walked away from a problem and then "out of the blue" realized the answer?

This Aha! or Eureka moment is a common experience, but have you ever thought about what causes this?

Incubation

Incubation is a process of unconscious recombination of thought elements stimulated through conscious work at one point in time, resulting in novel ideas later.

This means that taking a break and stopping with consciously working on a problem for a set period can help get a new insight that can solve the problem. On top of that, studies show that combining incubation with higher levels of dopamine (a neurotransmitter) increases our chances of having a great idea.

Because every time we do something enjoyable, more dopamine is released in our brains. You now have a perfect excuse to take that extra shower or going for a run!

RECAP

After reading this chapter, you should have some new tools and ideas at your disposal. First, we looked at some common pitfalls. We learned about the noise-to-signal ratio and how it increases as you consume more data. Another common pitfall is to make up your mind prior to looking at the facts before concluding a cause.

Then we discussed some troubleshooting tools. Binary search is an excellent technique for speeding up the process of elimination. With the Internet at your fingertips, a great troubleshooter should have excellent searching skills. We looked at some techniques to up your search skills. And because changes are often the cause of issues, we've also looked at a method to analyze changes.

I've shared some tips and tricks for what to do when you're stuck. When and how to get help by escalating a problem and how to use a rubber duck with troubleshooting.

Lastly, we saw how simplicity can be your friend and how to get more out of your Aha! moment!

CLOSING THOUGHTS

*"Problem-solving is a skill. You
learn more every day."*

Troubleshooting is the ability to diagnose and resolve a problem. One of the most challenging skills to acquire in an IT role isn't technical knowledge but effective troubleshooting.

With rapid developments in Artificial Intelligence and automation, I believe this will be more and more common. For all of us IT professionals, it becomes increasingly important to focus on future-proof *skills*. One of those skills is effective troubleshooting or problem-solving.

By reading this book, I hope you gained a new perspective on troubleshooting. It's an ongoing process to develop a skill. The information in this book will give you a head start, but it's up to you to take the lead, put it into practice and become a smarter troubleshooter!

Here's a quick summary of all the parts:

Part 1 introduces troubleshooting. It starts with having the right mindset, using your time and energy for creative troubleshooting. We also talked about what essential prerequisites we have to solve a problem and a basic one-size-fits-all approach.

Part 2 discusses the different troubleshooting strategies out there and where they differ. This will give us some background information about the basic problem-solving strategies to grasp troubleshooting better.

In part 3, we look at the IDEAL model. Following this model can help to generate creative solutions and give some structure for troubleshooting complex issues. In addition, you can become more aware of the steps that are needed to solve complex problems.

Finally, in part 4, we dive into some more practical stuff. We look at how to protect against some common pitfalls and show some tips and tricks to help you through tricky times when you're stuck.

I hope you found this book helpful, and I wish you all the best in your troubleshooting journey.

A little request

Thanks again for reading this book.

If you enjoyed it, I'd be super grateful if you left a review about it.

Thanks,

Bart

Printed in Great Britain
by Amazon